RACING CARS

IAN GRAHAM

Heinemann
LIBRARY

www.heinemann.co.uk/library
Visit our website to find out more information about **Heinemann Library** books.

To order:
☎ Phone 44 (0) 1865 888066
▤ Send a fax to 44 (0) 1865 314091
▢ Visit the Heinemann Bookshop at www.heinemann.co.uk/library to browse our catalogue and order online.

First published in Great Britain by Heinemann Library, Halley Court, Jordan Hill, Oxford OX2 8EJ, part of Harcourt Education.
Heinemann is a registered trademark of Harcourt Education Ltd.

Editorial: Andrew Farrow and Dan Nunn
Design: Jo Hinton-Malivoire and Tinstar Design Limited (www.tinstar.co.uk)
Illustrations: Geoff Ward
Picture Research: Rebecca Sodergren and Bob Battersby
Production: Viv Hichens
Originated by Dot Gradations Ltd
Printed and bound in China by South China Printing Company

ISBN 0 431 16562 9
07 06 05 04 03
10 9 8 7 6 5 4 3 2 1

British Library Cataloguing in Publication Data
Graham, Ian, 1953–
    Racing Cars. – (Designed for success)
    1. Automobiles, Racing – Juvenile literature
    I. Title
    629.2'28
A full catalogue record for this book is available from the British Library.

Acknowledgements
The publishers would like to thank the following for permission to reproduce photographs:
Auto Cars p. **28**; EPA pp. **5** (top), **6**, **13** (bottom), **15** (bottom); Corbis pp. **19** (bottom), **25** (bottom); Eye Ubiquitous/Darren Maybury p. **18**; Ferrari p. **15** (top); Formula 1 Pictures pp. **11** (bottom), **12**; Jeff Burk p. **23** (bottom); LAT p. **13** (top); LAT/Clive Rose p. **9** (top); LAT/Charles Coates pp. **8**, **25** (top); LAT/Gavin Lawrence p. **11** (top); LAT/Lorenzo Bellanca pp. **4**, **19** (top); LAT/M Levitt p. **7** (top); National Motor Museum pp. **26**, **27** (top), **29**; NHRA pp. **22**, **23** (top); PA Photos pp. **1**, **3**, **10**; Popperfoto pp. **14**, **20**, **21** (top), **22** (bottom), **24**; Power Stock p. **5** (bottom); Sutton Images pp. **9** (bottom), **16**, **27** (bottom).

Cover photograph reproduced with permission of Sutton Images.

Every effort has been made to contact copyright holders of any material reproduced in this book. Any omissions will be rectified in subsequent printings if notice is given to the publishers.

Disclaimer
All the Internet addresses (URLs) given in this book were valid at the time of going to press. However, due to the dynamic nature of the Internet, some addresses may have changed, or sites may have ceased to exist since publication. While the author and publishers regret any inconvenience this may cause readers, no responsibility for any such changes can be accepted by either the author or the publishers.

CONTENTS

Any words appearing in the text in bold, **like this**, are explained in the Glossary.

People have raced cars for more than 100 years. Since the very first race, designers and engineers have tried everything to make their cars go faster than all the others.

A racing car not only has to **accelerate** very quickly, it also has to remain **stable** at all speeds and corner fast without skidding or spinning. In search of faster acceleration and higher speeds, designers develop new engines, use new materials and try different body shapes. Compared to a family car, a racing car usually has a more powerful engine, a lower, more lightweight body, a sleeker shape and bigger rear tyres. It also **handles** better than a family car. Many of the best racing car design ideas, including improved engines, brakes and tyres, are later built into ordinary family cars.

SINGLE-SEATERS

International single-seat racing is divided into different classes, or formulas. These include **Formula 1** (shown here), **Formula 3000** and **Formula 3**. The 'formula' is a list of rules covering the car's size, weight, engine and fuel. The formulas are intended to make sure that all the cars in a race are similar to each other and so the race will be exciting to watch.

SPORTS CARS

The term 'sports car' can be used to describe a range of cars. Some sports cars are passenger cars that are designed to be fun to drive on the open road. They have more power for their weight and better handling than the average passenger car. Other sports cars are used specially for racing. Some are almost identical to road-going models. Others are racing versions of road cars. They look like road cars, but have been completely rebuilt to be faster. There are also high-tech sports cars designed from scratch as ultra-fast racing cars.

SALOONS AND STOCKS

Saloon cars are also known as 'touring cars', 'stock cars' or 'sedans'. There are races for saloon cars.

- Some racing saloon cars are almost standard models. The only difference is that they carry some extra safety equipment.
- Other racing saloon cars look like standard **production cars**, but underneath their familiar-looking body they are specially built racing machines.

RULE-MAKERS

The rules and regulations for each type of motor racing are set by organizations or governing bodies. The FIA (Fédération Internationale de l'Automobile) regulates Formula 1 racing. **NASCAR** (the National Association for Stock Car Auto Racing) controls stock car racing in the USA. **CART** (Championship Auto Racing Teams) is the organization behind the **Champ car** championship (see pages 6–7).

CHAMP CARS

The **CART Champ Car** championship is the leading American single-seat motor racing sport. Champ cars are the fastest circuit-racing cars in the world. A Champ car's body is slung low between its wheels instead of sitting on top of them. The engine is placed behind the driver. The big, broad rear wheels are driven by the engine, while the smaller front wheels steer the car. **Wings** at the front and back of the car create downforce (downward **air pressure**). This allows the car to go round bends faster. To keep the car's body close to the ground, the driver sits low in the car with a seat that leans back into the **cockpit**. A Champ car weighs less than half as much as a typical family car, but has a far more powerful engine. The combination of its light weight, high **horsepower** engine and **streamlined** shape enables a Champ car to **accelerate** from zero to 160 kmph (100 mph) in under five seconds. It can reach an amazing top speed of almost 400 kmph (250 mph) on the fastest circuits.

BANK ON IT!

Champ cars fight for position in a high-speed dash for victory. Many of the tracks they compete on in the USA are oval-shaped with banked corners. A banked corner rises up higher towards the outside of the corner. The banking enables the cars to corner much faster than they could on a flat track.

Gil de Ferran of Brazil leads the field in his Honda/Reynard CART, September 2001.

FILL HER UP!

A Champ car takes on **fuel** through a hose that plugs into the car. A second hose at the top lets air and dangerous fumes out safely as fuel fills the tank. Champ cars do not burn ordinary petrol in their engines. Instead, they burn a type of alcohol called methanol. It produces more power from the engine than petrol.

Newman/Haas Racing Champ car

Engine size: 2.65 litres

Engine type: V8 turbocharged

Engine power: 850 hp

Length: 4.9 metres

Weight: 700 kg

Top speed: 400 kmph (250 mph)

SPROUTING WINGS

Single-seat racing cars have wings at the front and back. The wings are shaped like an aeroplane's wing. When an aeroplane's wings cut through the air, they force air to travel further and faster over the curved top than the flatter underside. This lowers the air pressure above the wing. This difference in air pressure above and below the wing sucks the wing upwards.

Racing car designers turned this special wing shape, called an aerofoil, upside down so that it sucks the car downwards. This produces downforce, which gives the car more grip so it can corner faster without skidding.

downforce pushes the car downwards

wing

Racing versions of family cars compete with each other on the racetrack. In Europe and Australia, they're called touring cars or saloons. In the USA, they're called stock cars or sedans.

Racing saloons look like standard **production cars**, but many of them are rebuilt especially for racing. Inside, these cars look completely different from a family car. Nothing is fitted to the car that is not needed for racing. All the soft padding that normally lines the roof and doors is stripped out. There is only one seat, for the driver. Like all racing car drivers, saloon drivers wear a fireproof suit, helmet and full racing harness, and sit inside a strengthened **roll cage** for protection. Strict rules apply to the cars that are allowed to enter the various saloon car races. The rules cover the design of the cars and the engines they can use.

AUSTRALIAN SUPERCARS

Australian manufactured cars, mainly Ford Falcons and Holden Commodores, dominate Australian touring car racing. There are two main types of Australian touring cars. The smaller 'supertourers' are powered by 2-**litre** engines. The main attractions, though, are the bigger **V8** supercars, with their more powerful 5-litre engines.

A pair of Holden V8 Supercars race to the finish line at Melbourne in Australia.

GERMAN TOURING RACERS

Many countries have their own touring car championships. Germany has the Deutsche Tourenwagen Masters, or DTM for short. The 2001 championship was won by a Mercedes CLK-DTM.

US SUPER STOCKS

NASCAR stock cars are quite unlike any road car. Each one is hand-built to particular requirements. Under the bonnet, there is an enormous V8 5.8 litre engine. On the roof, there are flaps that stand up if the car goes into a high-speed spin. They are designed to spoil the car's **streamlined** shape so that there is no danger of it taking off like an aircraft! The driver's side window is covered by nylon netting to stop wreckage from flying inside during a crash. The netting also keeps the driver's arms safely inside the car.

Chevrolet Monte Carlo NASCAR stock car

Engine size: 5.8 litres

Engine type: V8

Engine power: 700 hp

Length: 5.0 metres

Weight: 1545 kg

Top speed: 320 kmph (200 mph)

FERRARI F2002
FERRARI FLAIR

The Italian car maker Ferrari is world-famous for creating beautifully styled high-**performance** road cars. Its racing cars are winners too. When the great Italian driver Alberto Ascari won his first **Formula 1** world championship in 1952, he was driving a Ferrari. Fifty years later another Ferrari driver, Michael Schumacher, ended the 2002 Formula 1 season as world champion.

The car he drove was the most advanced car Ferrari had created so far. The shape of its parts and the materials they were made from were carefully chosen to make the car as light and as **streamlined** as possible. The engine was specially designed for the car. The first step in the design process was to develop the car's shape using a CAD (computer aided design) system. Then models and full-size cars were built and tested in a wind tunnel. Next, prototype (test model) cars were built and tested with the new engine. Finally, the racing cars themselves were built.

air intake

cockpit

engine

rear wing

rear-view mirror

The F2002 is the 48th single-seat racing car built by Ferrari for the Formula 1 world championship.

side pod

front wing

AERODYNAMICS

The shape and **aerodynamics** of the F2002 were refined during months of tests in a wind tunnel. An aircraft engine blows air through the tunnel to **simulate** the car travelling at different speeds. **Sensors** all over the car show the forces that act on different parts of it. The way air flowed around every part of the new Ferrari was studied. Designers wanted to see if it could be improved by changing the angle of one part or the size of another. Even the shape of the driver's helmet was designed according to tests in the wind tunnel.

A Formula 1 car model is tested in a wind tunnel. All Formula 1 manufacturers, including Ferrari, use wind tunnels to test the aerodynamics of their cars.

POWERPLANT

Ferrari developed a new engine for the F2002. The new Model 051 engine is made from aluminium, a very light metal, to save weight. A computer, called an 'engine management system', controls the engine to make sure that it always works at its best. Engineers can change the way the system runs the engine to suit the conditions at different racetracks.

FERRARI F2002

MADE BY HAND

To make their Formula 1 car, the Ferrari racing team has to assemble nearly 10,000 parts and more than a kilometre of wire!

Most family cars are made from steel. Formula 1 cars are made from different materials, such as aluminium, **carbon fibre** and **titanium**, which are lighter and stronger than steel. The most important part of the car is the carbon fibre 'tub' that the driver sits in for protection. As well as being strong, carbon fibre can withstand very high temperatures. For this reason it is also used to make parts of the car's braking system, which can reach 1300° Celsius during a race. When most cars are built, they stay the same from then on. Formula 1 cars are constantly being altered to suit the different conditions at different racetracks. The engine settings, **suspension**, **gearbox** and **wing** angles are all changed to make the car as fast as possible.

MAKING AN F1 CAR

Thousands of family cars are built on **assembly lines,** where robots often do some of the work. Ferrari F2002s were each built by hand by a team of engineers. They work in a room almost as clean as a hospital operating theatre!

CARBON FIBRE

Carbon fibre starts as threads of rayon, a man-made fibre usually used to make clothes. The rayon is heated to 2600° Celsius to change it into carbon. The carbon fibres are woven together to make something that looks like black cloth. To make a car part, the cloth is laid in a mould, soaked with a liquid called **resin** and cooked to harden the resin. The result is a material that, weight for weight, is five times stronger than steel.

A driver tries out a newly made carbon fibre body part at a Formula 1 factory.

SITTING PRETTY

A Formula 1 racing car corners so fast that the driver is pushed sideways with a force up to five times stronger than gravity. A close-fitting seat is very important, to hold the driver steady during a race. In fact, each seat is moulded to the exact shape of the driver's back to make sure that it's a perfect fit.

FERRARI F2002
RED HOT

A Formula 1 racing team like Ferrari spends hundreds of hours testing a new car to perfect its performance.

The Ferrari F2002 was developed from the F2001, the car with which Michael Schumacher won 9 of the 17 **Grand Prix** races in 2001. It was thoroughly tested on racetracks so its designers and engineers could fine-tune its engine and suspension to get the best possible performance. However, the real test comes when a car has to race against other cars. Within 2.5 seconds of the start, it is doing 100 kmph (60 mph). As it **accelerates**, the driver changes gear in a fraction of a second by pressing special switches called 'paddles' on the steering wheel. On the fastest straights, the car can reach 350 kmph (220 mph).

PIT STOPS
Formula 1 racing cars are designed to have their wheels replaced and **fuel** tank refilled in a few seconds. A stop for this during a race is called a **pit stop**. A trained crew of twenty or so people can fit four new wheels and refill the fuel tank in less than eight seconds!

HOT RUBBER

A car's tyres grip the track better when they are hot because the rubber softens as it warms up. Just before a race starts, the tyres are wrapped in specially made electric blankets. These bring the tyres up to the right temperature, about 90° Celsius. As the cars drive around the track to the starting grid, they swerve from side to side to keep the tyres hot. Spare wheels that will be fitted to the car during a pit stop are also heated beforehand to give maximum grip.

THE RACE FOR DATA

During a race, each car sends information to its team at the trackside by radio. More than 100 sensors all over the car measure everything from the temperatures of various parts to the tyre pressures and engine speed. About three **megabytes** of **data** (enough to fill two floppy discs) are transmitted every lap. The team sees precisely how its cars are performing. If anything worries them, they can radio a warning to the car's driver or ask him to come into the **pits**.

Ferrari F2002
Formula 1 car

Engine size: 3 litres

Engine type: V10

Engine power: 860 hp

Length: 4.4 metres

Weight (with driver): 600 kg

Top speed: 350 kmph (220 mph)

ENGINES

A racing car engine works in the same way as a typical family car's engine, but a racing engine is lighter and more powerful.

In theory, a racing car engine does a very simple job. It burns **fuel** to release the **chemical energy** stored inside it. It then uses this energy to drive the car's wheels. In practice, racing car engines are amazingly complicated. They can have up to twelve **cylinders**, compared to a small family car's four cylinders. Each cylinder needs its own supply of fuel and air, and an electrical supply to make the sparks that **ignite** the fuel. **Valves** have to open and close dozens of times a second to let air in and waste gas out at precisely the right moment. Oil moves through the engine to make sure that all the moving parts slide easily, and water cools the engine. The whole process is controlled by a computer.

WHERE IS THE ENGINE?

Racing cars often have their engine behind the driver. Placing the engine in this position lets the designer make the front of the car lower or narrower, so that it's **streamlined**. It also puts the weight of the engine closer to the middle of the car, which makes the car easier to **handle**.

engine position

SUCK, SQUEEZE, BANG, BLOW

A racing engine works in a series of four steps. They are often called suck, squeeze, bang and blow. As each movement of the piston is called a 'stroke', this is also called the four-stroke cycle.

1 Induction stroke
The piston moves down the cylinder, inducting (sucking in) air through the open inlet valve.

2 Compression stroke
The inlet valve closes, fuel is sprayed in and the piston moves up the cylinder, compressing (squeezing) the mixture.

3 Power stroke
An electric spark ignites the fuel. The air expands and pushes the piston down the cylinder, providing the engine with power.

4 Exhaust stroke
The engine pushes the piston back up the cylinder, forcing the hot waste gases out through the open exhaust valve.

A turbocharged engine

air forced into engine

exhaust from engine

air in

blower   turbine

exhaust out

BOOSTING POWER

If an engine could burn more fuel, it would be more powerful. However, fuel burns only when it has enough oxygen from the air. There are two ways of forcing more air into the engine – turbocharging and supercharging. In a turbocharged engine (left), the hot **exhaust** gases leaving the engine spin a part like a propeller, called a turbine. This is linked to another turbine, called a blower. The blower is located in the pipe that sucks air into the engine. When this spins, it blows more air into the engine. A supercharger does the same thing, but it is driven directly by the engine instead of its exhaust gases.

Sports cars are small, low-slung cars built for speed and **manoeuvrability**. Some are designed to be driven on public roads. Others are specially designed for racing. They include some of the most beautiful racing cars that have ever been built.

The classic sports car for driving on public roads is a small open-topped two-seater. Larger sports cars built for higher speeds, with an enclosed **cockpit**, are known as GT cars. GT stands for '*gran turismo*' or 'grand touring'. Sports and GT racing cars are two-seaters too, although the passenger seat is not fitted. Most sports cars have their engine fitted at the front, but most modern racing sports cars have their engine mounted in the middle of the car. Sports cars have become more and more sophisticated over the years. Changes in design have included lowering the front of the car, making the body more **streamlined**, adding a **wing** at the back and replacing a lot of the metal parts with **carbon fibre**.

24 HOURS AT THE WHEEL

The most famous sports car race is held every year near Le Mans in France. Most motor races are 2 or 3 hours long, but the Le Mans sports car race lasts for 24 hours. It's called an endurance race. A team of drivers take turns to drive the car. The leading cars can reach 320 kmph (200 mph) on the circuit's long straights. Cars can average more than 200 kmph (125 mph) over the whole 24 hours. In that time, the winning car can cover more than 5000 kilometres. The cars have to be very reliable to run so fast for so long.

LE MANS AMERICAN STYLE

There is only one Le Mans 24-hour race, but the Le Mans cars can now be seen all over the world in the American Le Mans Series (ALMS). ALMS was created specially for these cars. They take part in twelve events in different countries. But none of the ALMS races are 24-hour marathons. Most of them only last for 165 minutes.

Audi R8 Le Mans sports car

Engine size: 3.6 litres

Engine type: V8 turbocharged

Engine power: 610 hp

Length: 4.6 metres

Weight: 900 kg

Top speed: about 350 kmph (220 mph)

CLASSIC RACERS

Old racing cars often find a new home in a museum when their racing days are over. Some of them carry on racing in events for classic cars. Graceful Jaguars from the 1950s (pictured right) and elegant Ferraris from the 1960s still take part in classic sports car races.

Rallying is one of the toughest tests of car and driver in motor sport. Rallies are held on closed roads and courses, called stages, set out in forests and parks.

A good rally car has to be an all-rounder – fast on the straights, quick and safe through the bends and **stable** over the bumps. And it has to do all of this on all sorts of road surfaces. Rally cars race on **asphalt**, concrete, gravel, mud and even snow and ice. The best rally drivers can reach an amazing 140 kmph (85 mph) on a twisting, slippery, icy course. While the driver concentrates on driving the car, a navigator in the passenger seat follows a map of the course. He or she shouts instructions to the driver through an **intercom** system built into their helmets. The cars look like ordinary family cars, but they are actually hand-built from scratch and are far from ordinary.

ROCK AND ROLL

Rally cars are probably more likely to end up upside-down than any other type of racing car. The driver and navigator sit inside a strong **roll cage**. This stops the roof from collapsing on them if the car rolls over. The cage is built from steel tubes welded together.

WORLD RALLY CHAMPIONSHIP

The cars that take part in the World Rally Championship are designed to be taken apart very quickly for repairs. Hitting a rock at high speed can shatter a wheel. However, the driver can fit a new wheel in less than five minutes. As soon as a car finishes a stage, a team of mechanics prepares it for the next stage. They can replace a part, even a major part such as a **gearbox**, within fifteen minutes.

Peugeot 206 World Rally car

Engine size: 2 litres

Engine type: 4-cylinder in-line turbocharged

Engine power: 300 hp

Length: 4.0 metres

Weight: 1230 kg

Top speed: 200 kmph (125 mph)

TYRE TROUBLES

Rally teams choose from a variety of different types of tyres, depending on the weather and the ground conditions.

- On dry, hard surfaces teams choose tyres that are almost completely smooth – these allow the car to go faster.
- On loose surfaces, such as gravel, they choose tyres with a chunky, knobbly **tread** that gives more grip.
- For snow and ice, they fit tyres covered with steel studs or spikes, like the one on the left.

Drag racing is the fastest and most exciting motor sport on Earth. Racing a drag car, or dragster, is more like strapping yourself into a rocket than driving a car!

Dragsters are designed to cover a straight track, usually a quarter of a mile (402 metres) long, in the shortest possible time. They **accelerate** faster than any other racing car. There are more than a dozen different types, or classes, of dragsters. The fastest, called the Top Fuel cars, leave the start line faster than a jet fighter-plane! In less than one second, they are doing 160 kmph (100 mph)! They have the most powerful engines in racing for punching their long thin bodies along the track. They measure their power in thousands of **horsepower**. The cars race two at a time against the clock. The noise, as they blast down the track, is deafening and the ground shakes. A whole race, from start to finish, lasts just a few seconds!

FUEL RECIPES

Top Fuel dragster engines don't burn ordinary petrol. They burn a special fuel called nitromethane. Anyone working near a nitromethane car has to wear a gas mask because of the harmful fumes the engine produces. Apart from carbon monoxide, an invisible poisonous gas, it can also produce nitric acid – a strong acid that can even eat through metal.

KEEPING IT STRAIGHT

The design of a dragster makes it difficult to steer. When it roars away from the start line, the engine delivers so much power to the rear wheels that the front of the car tries to lift off the ground. Front wheels that are off the ground or that have very little grip cannot steer the car. If the nose begins to veer to one side, the force of the air suddenly hitting the side of the car can push it off-course in a moment.

SLOWING DOWN

The fastest dragsters need more than brakes to stop them at the end of a race. As they cross the finish line, they release a parachute from the back of the car. The broad sheet of material catches the air, slowing the car down.

Kenny Bernstein's Top Fuel dragster

Engine size: 8.2 litres

Engine type: V8 supercharged

Engine power: 6500 hp

Weight: 990 kg (with driver)

Top speed: 500+ kmph (310+ mph)

Safety is an important factor in the design of cars that race around a track at 350 kmph (220 mph) or more. Every care needs to be taken to protect the drivers and the thousands of spectators who watch them.

Motor racing is a dangerous sport. If something goes wrong, it often happens in the blink of an eye and the result can be disastrous. Racing car designers have to follow specially developed rules. These try to make the cars as safe as possible. Modern racing cars protect their drivers better than ever. The driver sits inside a 'survival cell'. This is designed to withstand the enormous forces of a crash without collapsing or crushing the driver. The tracks are safer now too. Many of them have wide 'run-off' areas and soft barriers designed to catch cars that leave a track. Motor racing, though still dangerous, is probably safer now than it has ever been and it is just as exciting to watch.

The start of a race is particularly dangerous as the cars **accelerate** hard very close together. Here, smokes pours from a car's tyres as the driver brakes hard to avoid a collision in front of him.

STRAPPING IN

The driver is tightly strapped into his or her seat by a harness. If the car crashes, the harness ensures that the driver stays inside the car's survival cell and is not thrown out. The straps are held together by one fastener in the middle. This lets the driver release them all in a fraction of a second and escape if necessary.

During a pit stop, the fuel cells can be filled within 6.5 seconds.

RUBBER TANKS

Racing cars are fitted with **fuel** tanks, called fuel cells, that look more like rubber bags. These strengthened bags are filled with plastic foam to stop the fuel from sloshing about or spraying out if the car crashes. **Valves** control the flow of fuel to the engine, and snap shut automatically to stop leaks. This greatly reduces the danger of fire.

SAFETY STANDARDS

Thanks to modern safety standards, drivers can survive crashes that would have killed them just a few years ago. In the early days of motor racing, drivers sat in open cockpits without seat belts. They wore cotton overalls that gave them no protection from the fires that often broke out after crashes. Many famous and successful drivers died on the track in those days. The Formula 1 champion driver Jackie Stewart played an important part in making motor racing as safe as it is today.

All racing car designers are constantly looking for new ideas to give their team's cars the edge over all the others. Of course, some ideas are more successful than others!

Most new racing cars improve a little on other existing cars. However, from time to time, a designer tries something completely new to leap ahead of everyone else. Some new ideas, such as putting the engine behind the driver or using **wings**, work so well that other teams copy them. However, many other new ideas are quickly dropped or banned. Racing car designers, especially in **Formula 1**, play a cat and mouse game with the rule-makers. The designers constantly push technology to the limit to make their cars faster. Meanwhile, the rule-makers constantly update the rules. Their aim is to keep all the cars as safe as possible and make sure they all have roughly the same **performance**. Some new designs fail to catch on simply because they do not live up to the designer's hopes for them.

JET-CARS

In the 1960s, several designers produced racing cars powered by **jet engines**. The first one nearly won the 1967 Indianapolis 500 race in the USA. The following year, the Lotus team raced four jet-cars in the USA. Two of them are pictured here. In 1971, Lotus also raced the only Formula 1 jet-car. The cars ran well at high speeds, but they could not **accelerate** as fast as other cars and the engines overheated when the cars slowed down.

SIX-WHEELERS

In 1976, the Tyrell Formula 1 team raced a car with six wheels. Two pairs of front wheels could be made smaller than one pair. Air flowed over the top of the small wheels more smoothly. However, both pairs of front wheels had to turn to steer the car. This made the front of the car very complicated and heavy. It failed to work as well as expected, and so the team went back to cars with four wheels the next year.

THE FAN CAR

In 1978, the Brabham Formula 1 team built a car with a big fan at the back. The spinning fan sucked air from underneath the car to suck the whole car down closer to the track. However, cars were not allowed to have moving parts that changed the way air flowed around them. The fan seemed to break this rule. Drivers also complained that it sucked up dirt and blew it at following cars, so the fan car had to go!

Every racing car is designed with a particular type of driver or sport in mind. This table of information compares the basic specifications and **performance** of some of today's best-known racing cars.

Car	Engine	Power (horsepower)	Weight (kilograms)	Top speed (kmph / mph)
Audi R8 Le Mans sports car	3.6-litre V8 (T)	610	900	350 / 220
Chevrolet Monte Carlo stock car	5.8-litre V8	700	1545	320 / 200
Ferrari F2002 Formula 1 car	3-litre V10	860	600 *	350 / 220
Holden Commodore VX V8 Supercar	5-litre V8	620	1350	300 / 190
Kenny Bernstein's Top Fuel dragster	8.2-litres V8 (S)	6500	990 *	500+ / 310+
Mercedes-Benz CLK-DTM	4-litre V8	470	1350	300 / 190
Newman/Haas Racing Champ car	2.65-litre V8 (T)	850	700	400 / 250
Peugeot 206 World Rally car	2-litre in-line 4 (T)	300	1230	200 / 125

T = Turbocharged   S = Supercharged   * includes weight of driver

THE FIRST MOTOR RACE

The first motor race was held in France in 1894. It wasn't supposed to be a race at all. It was called a trial. However, everyone wanted to know which car was the fastest. Count Jules de Dion's steam tractor won, but was disqualified. Next came Georges Lemaître in his Peugeot. The trial was so successful that a race was organized for the next year. Motor racing had begun.

This is a photograph of the Tour de France motor race in 1899.

FURTHER READING AND RESEARCH

BOOKS

Big Book of Racing, by Trevor Lord, Dorling Kindersley, 2001
Racing Cars, by David Jefferis, Belitha Press, 2001
Racing Cars, by Jon Kirkwood, Franklin Watts, 2001
Racing Cars, by C. Maynard, Franklin Watts, 1999

WEBSITES

http://news.bbc.co.uk/sport/hi/english/motorsport/default.stm
BBC Sport's motor sport section, which includes news, facts and features on motor racing and rallying.

http://www.nascar.com
The website of NASCAR, organizer of the US Winston Cup stock car championship.

http://www.cart.com
The website of CART, organizer of the US Champ car championship.

http://www.nhra.com
The website of the NHRA, organizer of US drag-racing championships.

http://www.howstuffworks.com
A website full of explanations of how things work, including NASCAR racing cars and CART Champ cars.

http://www.themotorweb.com.au
A website full of useful information about all aspects of motor racing in Australia.

The Cooper Climax car in 1959. It was the first Formula 1 car to have its engine behind the driver.

accelerate go faster. To make a racing car go faster, the driver presses the accelerator pedal. This feeds more fuel into the engine, which speeds up.

aerodynamics the science of how objects move through air. It is used in motor racing to design a car shape that slices through air quickly.

air pressure the pressing force of the air around us. Racing car wings are designed to lower the air pressure below them and suck the car downwards.

asphalt a mixture of black, tarry bitumen and gravel, used to make roads

assembly line a line of machines where workers or robots put cars together

carbon fibre material made from strands of carbon embedded in hard plastic. It is a very strong and lightweight material that is used to make parts of some sports cars and racing cars instead of steel.

CART Championship Auto Racing Teams, the US organization that sets the rules and regulations for several motor racing championships, including the FedEx CART Championship that Champ cars compete for

Champ car racing car that takes part in the CART Champ car races (Champ cars used to be called Indycars)

chemical energy the energy stored inside a chemical fuel such as petrol. The energy, released by burning the fuel, is used to make a car move.

cockpit the part of an aeroplane or car where the pilot or driver sits

cylinder tube-shaped part of a car engine where the fuel is burned

data information, especially in a form that can be used by a computer

exhaust the waste gases produced when an engine burns fuel

Formula 1 the leading international single-seat racing championship

Formula 3 a class of single-seat motor-racing

Formula 3000 international championship set up to give racing drivers experience in single-seaters before the best drivers move on to race in Formula 1

fuel substance that is burned inside an engine to provide the energy that drives the car's wheels

gearbox part of a racing car that feeds the engine power to the wheels. The engine drives one shaft and the wheels are driven by another shaft. The two shafts are linked by a set of gear-wheels with teeth that lock together. When the driver changes gear, a different gear-wheel links the two shafts, enabling the engine to drive the wheels over a wide range of speeds.

Grand Prix national race that counts towards an important championship such as the Formula 1 driver's championship

handling how a car responds and holds the road when it is being driven

horsepower unit of measurement of the power of an engine equal to the work done by one horse, or 746 watts of electrical power

ignite set on fire. The fuel inside an engine is set on fire by an electrical spark.

intercom a communication system that lets the driver and navigator hear each other over the noise of the engine

jet engines engines that work by burning fuel to create a high-speed stream, or jet, of gas, which makes a turbine spin. The turbine spins a fan that sucks air into the engine. Jet engines are also known as gas turbine engines.

litre measurement of capacity and a way of measuring the size of an engine. One litre is equivalent to 1000 cc (cubic centimetres).

manoeuvrability the ability to be steered nimbly and sharply

megabyte one megabyte is one million bytes of computer data. Each byte contains eight bits of information. A 'bit' is a zero or a one.

NASCAR the National Association for Stock Car Auto Racing, which sets the rules for the Winston Cup stock car championship

performance the way a vehicle functions – its speed, acceleration, stability, etc.

pit stop a short visit to the pits, during a race. Cars may come into the pits during a race to have new wheels fitted, their fuel tanks refilled (if allowed) or damaged parts replaced.

pits a row of garages beside the track, from where the race teams watch, refuel and fix their cars

production cars cars that are produced in large numbers for sale to the public

resin a liquid plastic used to make body parts of some racing cars. The plastic resin is poured into a mould. Mats of fibres made from glass or carbon are laid on top and soaked in the resin. When the resin sets, the result is a hard, smooth and lightweight part.

roll cage a protective frame made from steel tubes welded together

sensor a device that detects and measures something

simulate to recreate the effect of something

stable steady. A stable car keeps steady at all speeds.

streamlined designed to move through air very easily

suspension system of springs and shock absorbers that keep the body of a car relatively still while the wheels follow the bumps and hollows in the road

titanium a strong, lightweight metal that does not rust

tread the outer part of a tyre that touches the road

valve part of a racing car that opens and closes to start, stop and vary the flow of air, water or fuel through the engine

V8/V10 types of car engine. The number refers to the number of cylinders.

wings parts of a car shaped like upside down aircraft wings. As they cut through the air, they create a force that presses the car downwards.

INDEX